Beauty in Blurry

Photographs by Bottes du Roses

Dedicated to those who see differently

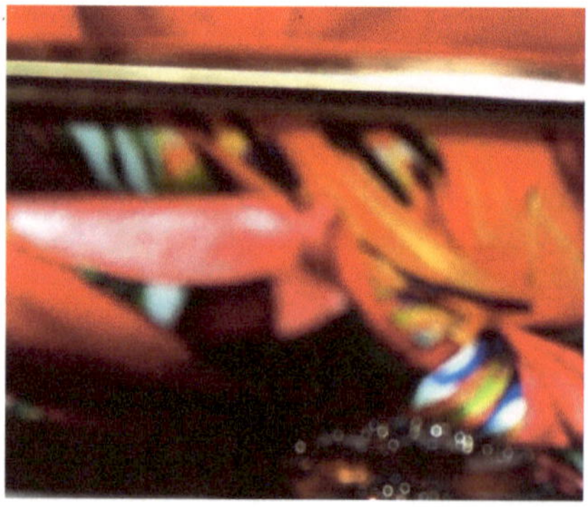

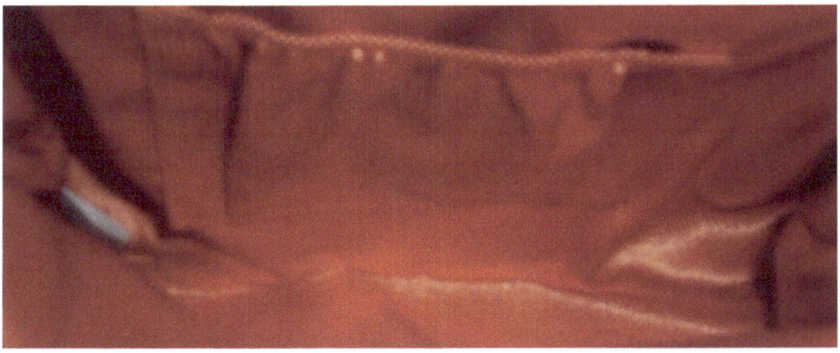

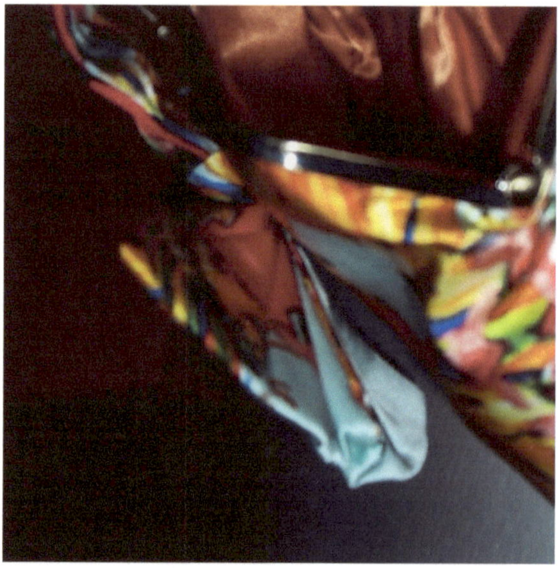

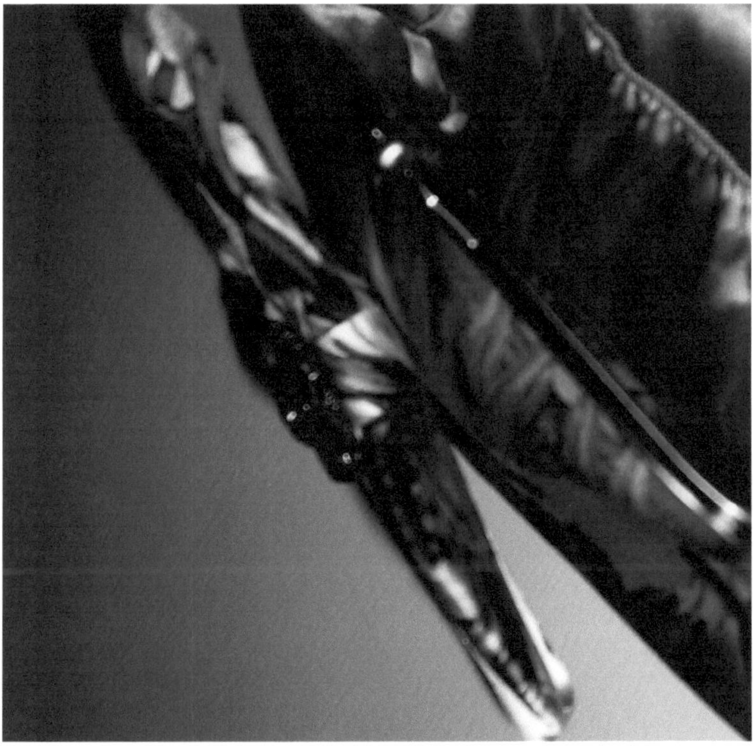

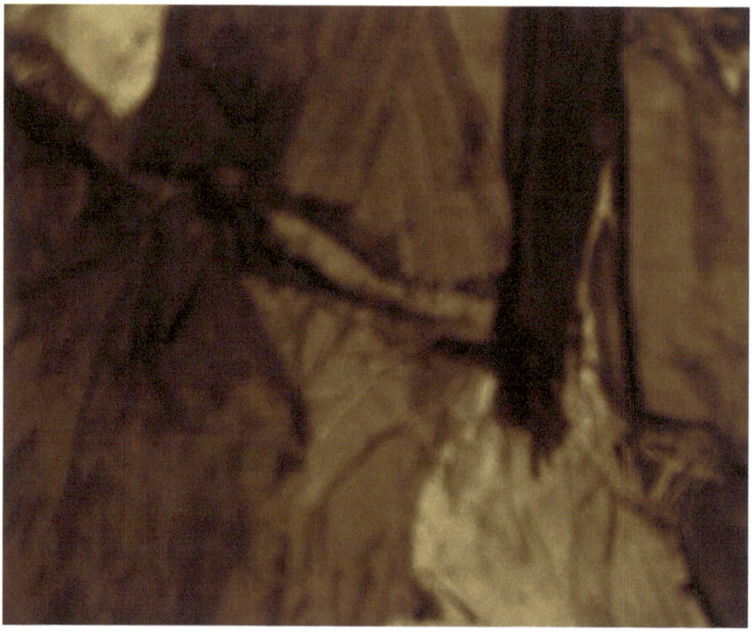

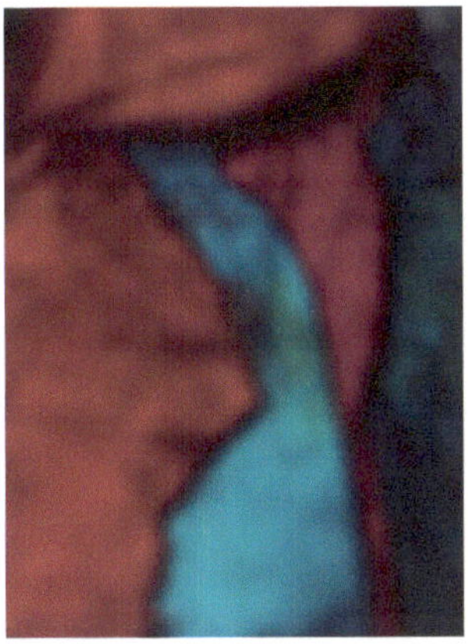

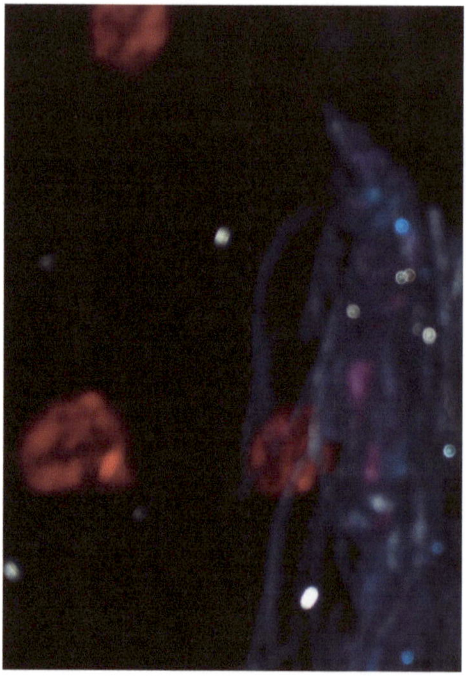

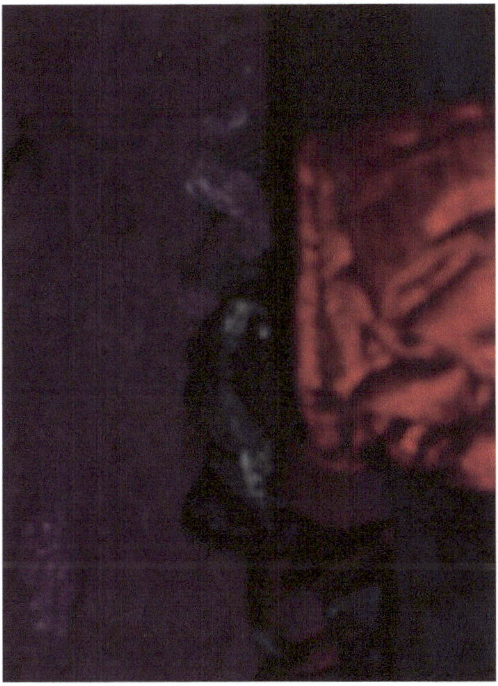

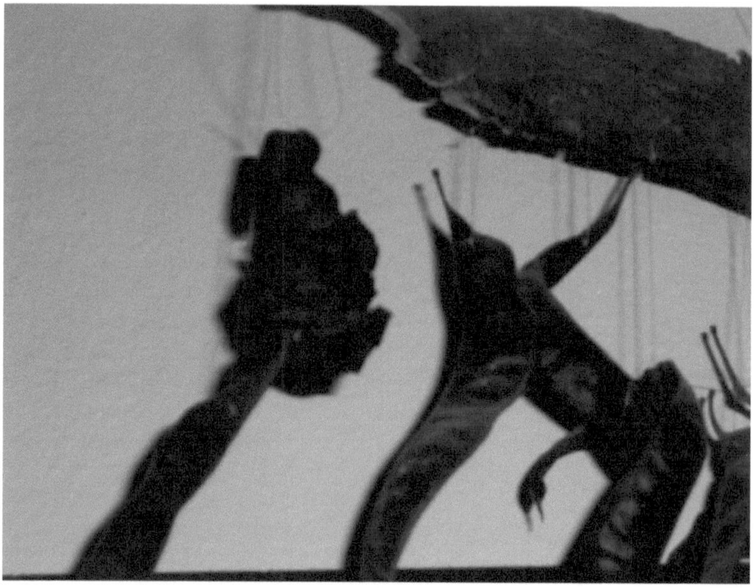

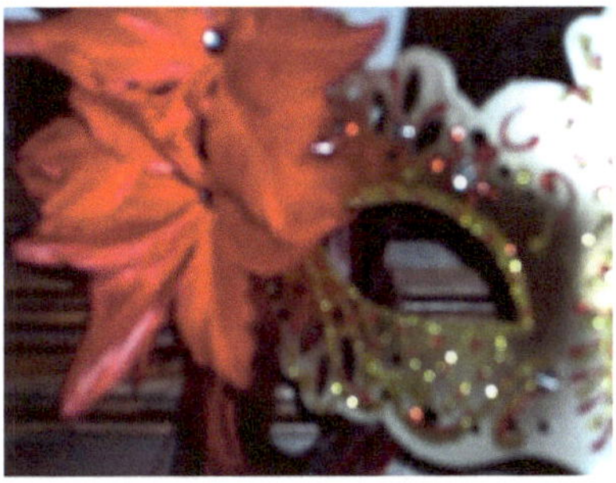

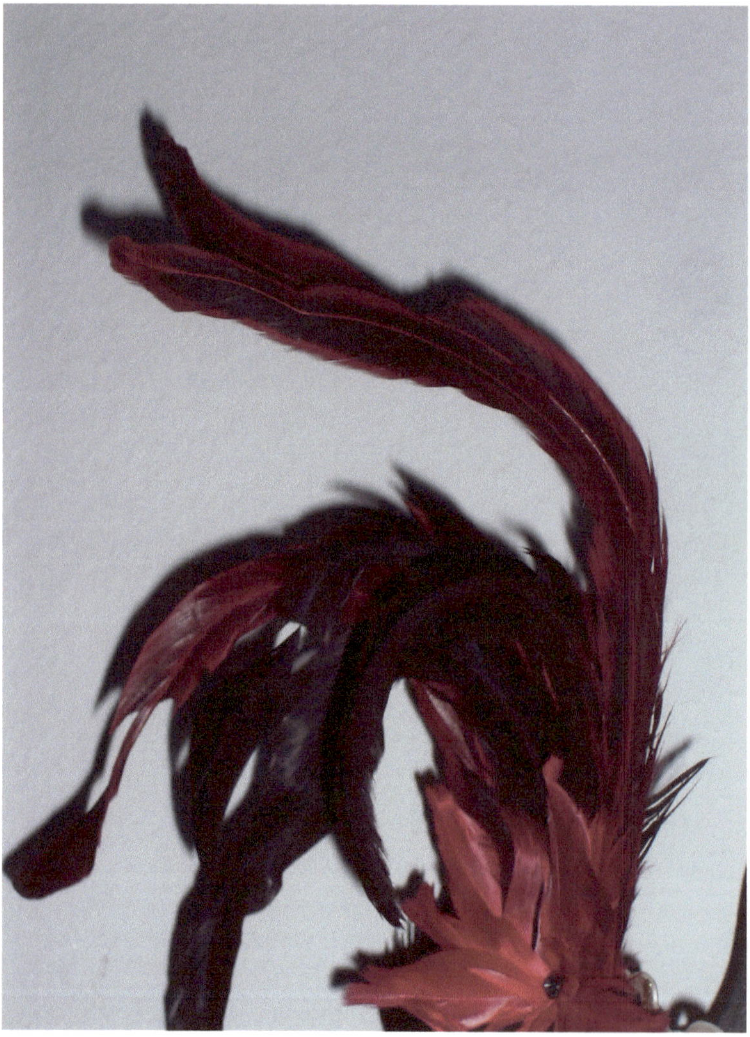

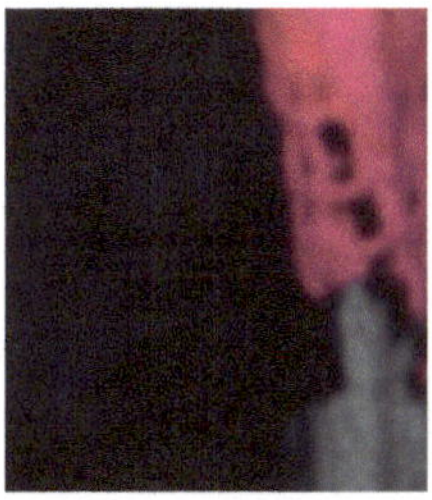

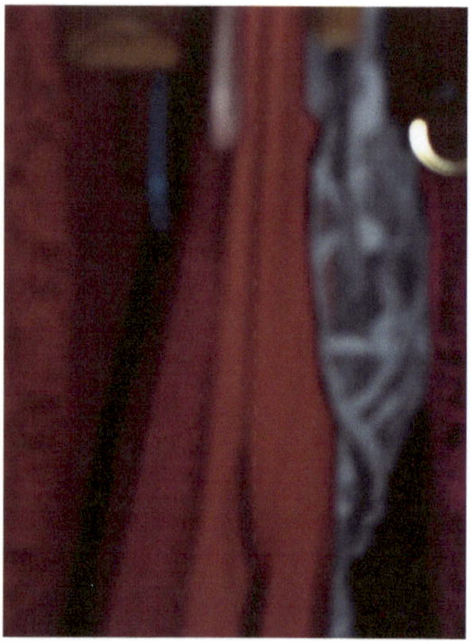

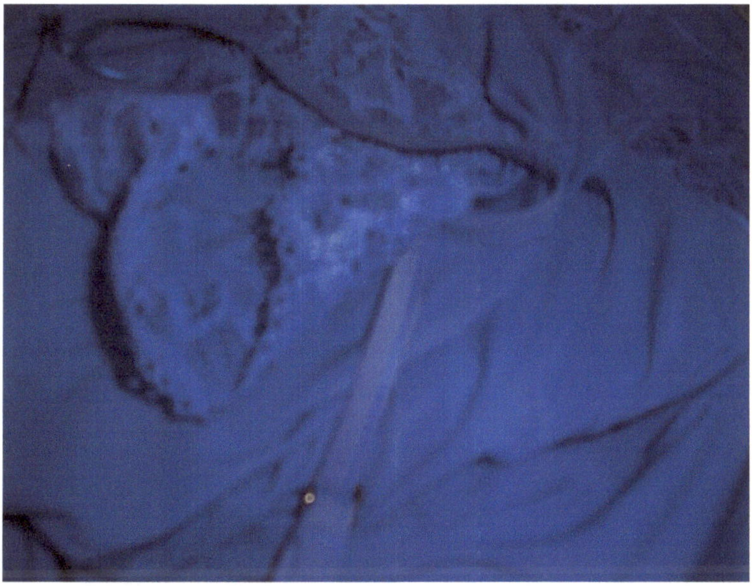

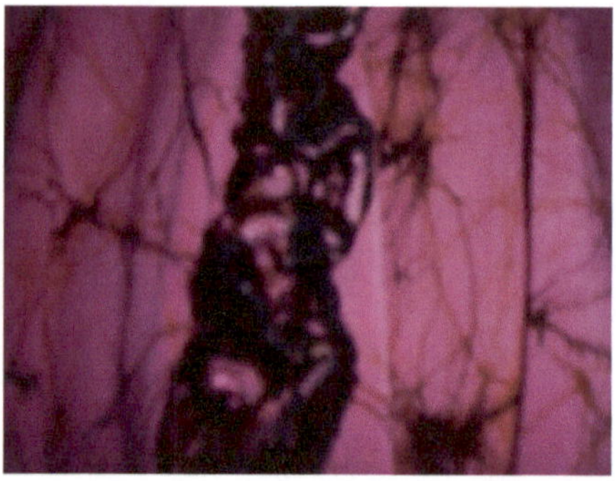

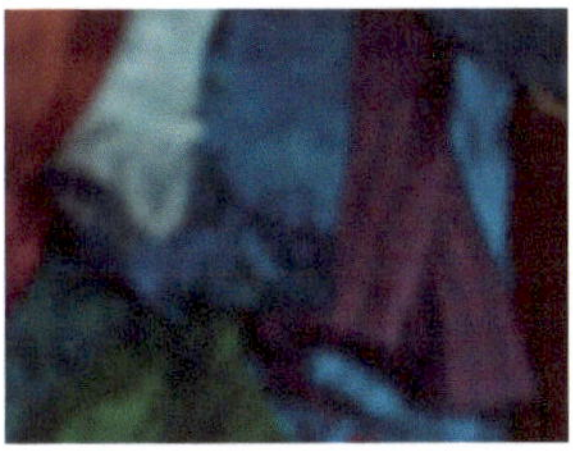

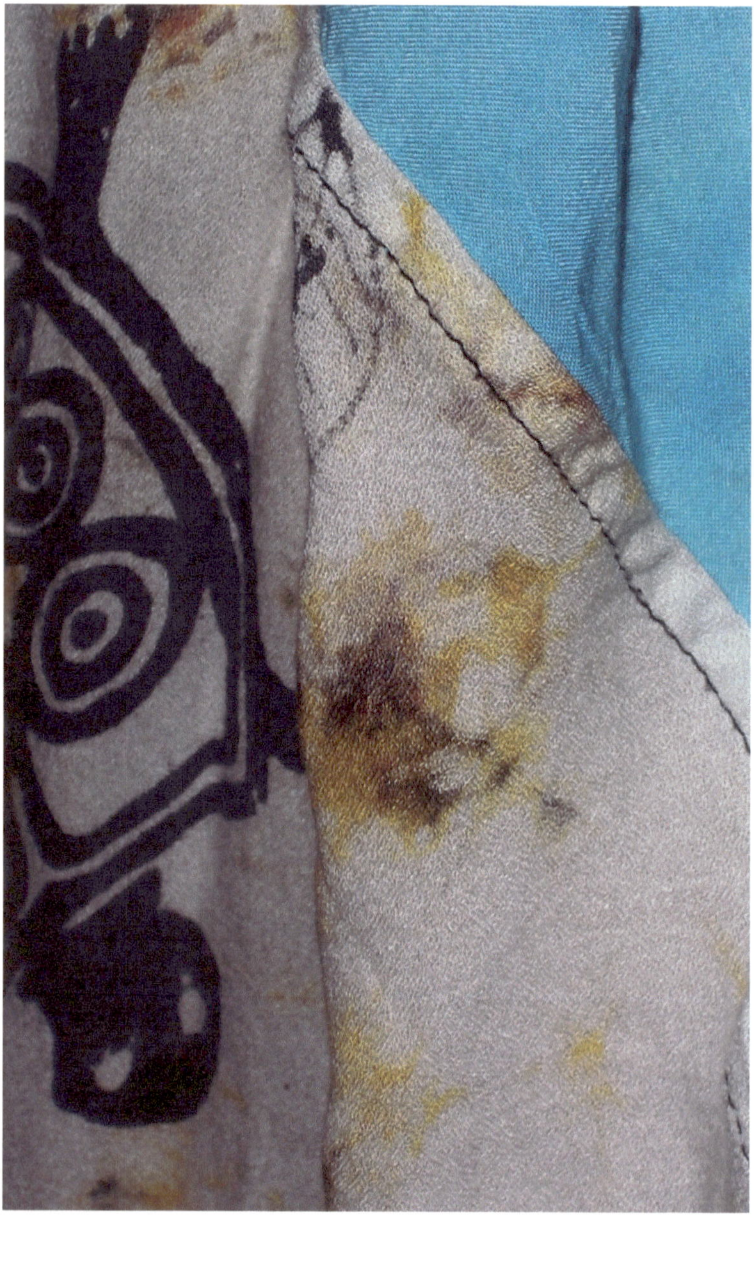

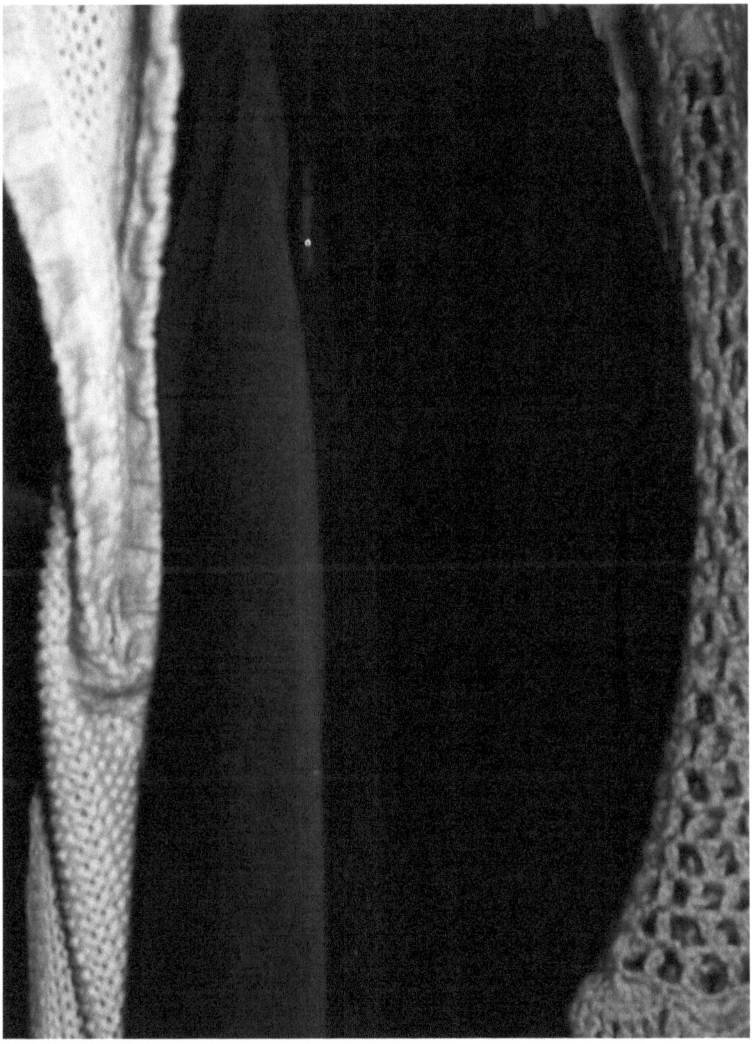

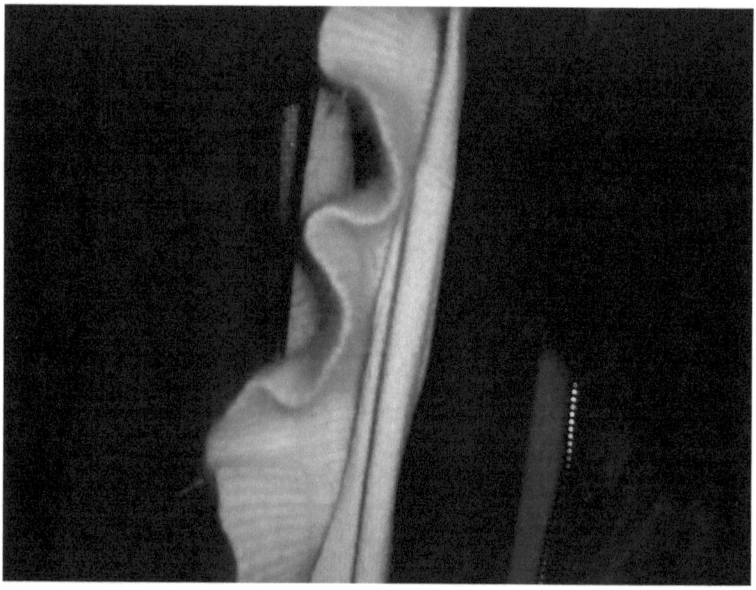

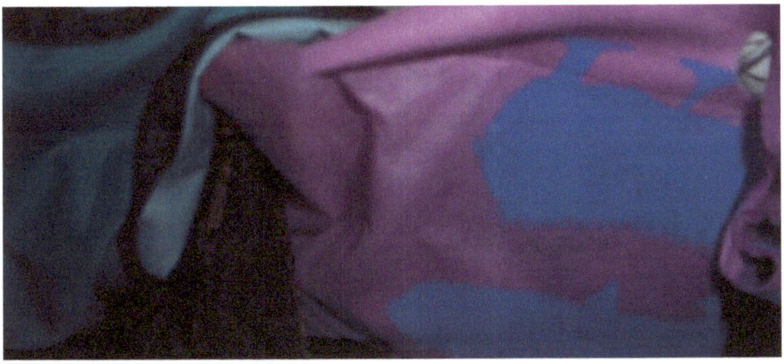

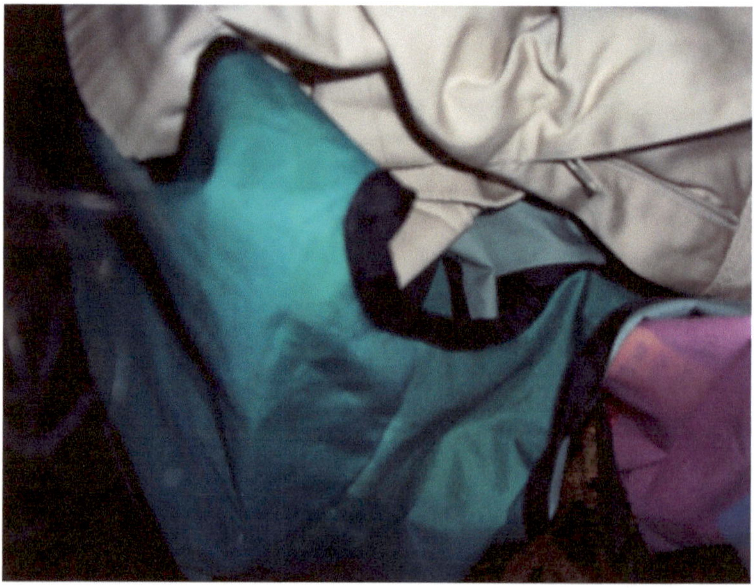

www.ingramcontent.com/pod-product-compliance
Lightning Source LLC
Chambersburg PA
CBHW041619180526
45159CB00002BC/925
9781501007293